SARA L. WESTON

Hidden Tales: Lesbians in Nordic Folklore

"In the heart of the North, where myths and legends intertwine with the very land itself, we embark on a journey of discovery. In the hidden corners of Nordic folklore, we find whispers of love and desire that defy time and tradition. This book delves into the enigmatic realms of lesbian representation in these age-old tales, shedding light on the hidden gems of love that have long been obscured by the shadows of history.

Sara

Contents

Foreword

Hidden Tales: Lesbians in Nordic Folklore is a groundbreaking exploration of the often overlooked stories of lesbian love and desire in the rich tapestry of Nordic mythology and folklore. Drawing from ancient sagas, legends, and folktales, this book uncovers the hidden narratives of same-sex relationships between women in the Nordic region. From the passionate love affairs of goddesses and valkyries to the forbidden romances of mortal women, these tales offer a unique perspective on the diverse expressions of love and sexuality in Norse, Icelandic, and Swedish folklore. Through careful research and analysis, this book sheds light on the presence and significance of lesbian characters and relationships in Nordic mythology, challenging traditional narratives and expanding our understanding of queer representation in folklore. Hidden Tales: Lesbians in Nordic Folklore is a must-read for anyone interested in LGBTQ+ history, mythology, and the power of storytelling to shape our understanding of identity and love.

1

Chapter 1

Introduction to Nordic Folklore

1.1 Overview of Nordic Folklore

Nordic folklore is a rich and diverse tapestry of myths, legends, and tales that have been passed down through generations in the Nordic countries of Scandinavia. These stories are deeply rooted in the cultural heritage of the region and provide a glimpse into the beliefs, values, and traditions of the people who inhabited these lands.

Nordic folklore encompasses a wide range of themes and characters, including gods and goddesses, mythical creatures, heroes, and supernatural beings. These stories often revolve around the natural world, with a particular emphasis on the harsh and unforgiving landscapes of the Nordic region. The folklore of the Nordic countries is closely intertwined with their history, geography, and climate, reflecting the challenges and triumphs of the people who lived there.

One of the fascinating aspects of Nordic folklore is its portrayal of women. While women have often been marginalized or overlooked in traditional narratives, Nordic folklore offers a unique perspective by featuring strong and complex female characters. These women are not merely passive figures but active participants in the stories, shaping the events and influencing the outcomes.

In Nordic folklore, women are often depicted as powerful beings with supernatural abilities. They can be goddesses, sorceresses, or mythical creatures, each with their own unique traits and roles. These female characters embody a range of qualities, including wisdom, strength, cunning, and beauty. They are not confined to traditional gender roles but are portrayed as multifaceted individuals who possess agency and make their own choices.

While the representation of women in Nordic folklore is significant, it is important to note that the stories have predominantly focused on heterosexual relationships. However, hidden within these tales are narratives that hint at the existence of same-sex relationships, including lesbian love.

Exploring the hidden tales of lesbians in Nordic folklore provides a fresh perspective on the stories and characters that have shaped the cultural identity of the region. By uncovering these narratives, we can challenge the heteronormative lens through which folklore has often been interpreted and create a more inclusive understanding of the past.

The presence of lesbians in Nordic folklore can be found in various mythological beings and figures. Valkyries, for example, are powerful female warriors who serve the gods and play a crucial role in Norse mythology. While their primary function is to choose the fallen warriors who will enter Valhalla, there are stories that suggest same-sex relationships among Valkyries.

The Norns, who are the weavers of fate in Nordic mythology, also offer glimpses of lesbian love. These three female figures control the destinies of both gods and humans, and their interactions with each other sometimes hint at romantic relationships.

Sea maidens, forest spirits, troll women, and witch women are other examples of mythological beings in Nordic folklore that have the potential to represent lesbian love. These characters often possess a sense of otherness and are associated with the natural world, which allows for the exploration of non-normative relationships.

By delving into these hidden tales, we can uncover the complexities of lesbian love in Nordic folklore and shed light on the diverse experiences and identities that have existed throughout history. These stories not only provide a sense of validation and representation for lesbian individuals but also challenge the notion that same-sex love is a modern phenomenon.

In the following chapters, we will explore the specific mythological beings mentioned earlier and delve into their stories and symbolism. By examining these narratives, we can gain a deeper understanding of the representation of lesbians in Nordic folklore and the significance of these tales in shaping lesbian identity and culture.

Through this exploration, we hope to inspire future generations to embrace their own identities and find solace in the rich tapestry of folklore that has been passed down through the ages. By recognizing and celebrating the hidden tales of lesbians in Nordic folklore, we can create a more inclusive and diverse understanding of our cultural heritage.

1.2 Importance of Folklore in Nordic Culture

Folklore plays a significant role in Nordic culture, serving as a window into the beliefs, values, and traditions of the people. It is a rich tapestry of stories, myths, and legends that have been passed down through generations, shaping the collective identity of the Nordic people. The importance of folklore lies in its ability to connect individuals to their cultural heritage, providing a sense of belonging and fostering a deeper understanding of their roots.

In Nordic societies, folklore has been a means of preserving history and cultural knowledge. Through oral tradition, stories have been shared and retold, ensuring that important lessons, customs, and beliefs are not forgotten. Folklore acts as a repository of wisdom, offering insights into the experiences, struggles, and triumphs of the past. It serves as a reminder of the resilience and resourcefulness of the Nordic people, as well as their deep connection to the natural world.

Furthermore, folklore serves as a source of entertainment and escapism. In a time before television and the internet, storytelling was a cherished pastime, bringing communities together and providing a form of shared entertainment. Folklore allowed people to immerse themselves in fantastical worlds, populated by mythical creatures, gods, and heroes. These stories provided a means of escape from the hardships of everyday life, offering a glimpse into a realm where anything was possible.

Folklore also plays a crucial role in shaping cultural values and norms. Through the tales of gods, goddesses, and legendary figures, societal expectations and moral codes are conveyed. These stories often contain lessons about bravery, loyalty, honor, and the consequences of one's actions. By internalizing these narratives, individuals are guided in their behavior and decision-making, contributing to the formation of a cohesive and harmonious society.

Moreover, folklore serves as a source of inspiration and creativity. The vivid imagery, colorful characters, and enchanting landscapes found in Nordic folklore have influenced countless artists, writers, and musicians throughout history. From the paintings of the Romantic era to contemporary literature and music, the themes and motifs of Nordic folklore continue to captivate and inspire creative minds. By drawing upon these rich traditions, artists are able to create works that resonate with audiences and evoke a sense of cultural pride.

In the context of lesbian representation, folklore takes on an even greater significance. For centuries, LGBTQ+ individuals have been marginalized and excluded from mainstream narratives. By exploring hidden tales of lesbians in Nordic folklore, we are reclaiming and amplifying the voices of those who have been silenced. These stories provide a sense of validation and visibility for lesbian individuals, offering a historical and cultural context for their identities.

By uncovering and sharing these hidden tales, we are challenging the heteronormative narratives that have dominated folklore for so long. We are expanding the boundaries of representation and creating a more inclusive understanding of Nordic culture. Lesbian characters in folklore serve as powerful symbols of resilience, love, and empowerment, offering a counter-narrative to the prevailing stereotypes and misconceptions surrounding LGBTQ+ individuals.

In conclusion, folklore holds immense importance in Nordic culture. It serves as a bridge between the past and the present, connecting individuals to their heritage and providing a sense of belonging. Folklore shapes cultural values, offers entertainment and inspiration, and acts as a repository of wisdom. By exploring hidden tales of lesbians in Nordic folklore, we are not only reclaiming marginalized voices but also challenging societal norms and fostering a more inclusive understanding of Nordic culture.

1.3 Representation of Women in Nordic Folklore

Nordic folklore is rich with tales of powerful and fascinating women who play significant roles in shaping the narratives and traditions of the region. These women are often portrayed as strong, independent, and wise, challenging traditional gender roles and expectations. While many of these stories focus on heterosexual relationships, there are also hidden tales that depict same-sex love and desire between women. These hidden tales provide a glimpse into the diverse and inclusive nature of Nordic folklore, highlighting the presence of lesbians in these ancient narratives.

In Nordic folklore, women are not merely passive characters or damsels in distress. They are often depicted as active partici-pants in the stories, possessing agency and making their own choices. These women are not confined to traditional gender roles but are instead portrayed as warriors, seers, and magical beings. Their strength and resilience are celebrated, and their actions have a profound impact on the outcome of the tales.

One of the reasons why women are represented so promi-nently in Nordic folklore is the importance of female deities and supernatural beings in the mythology of the region. Goddesses such as Freyja, the goddess of love and fertility, and Skadi, the goddess of winter and hunting, are revered and worshipped.

These goddesses embody various aspects of femininity, including sensuality, strength, and independence. Their stories often involve themes of love, desire, and power, providing a fertile ground for exploring same-sex relationships.

In addition to the goddesses, there are also other female supernatural beings in Nordic folklore who play significant roles in the representation of women. Valkyries, for example, are powerful warrior maidens who serve the gods and choose the slain warriors to bring to Valhalla. These fierce and fearless women are often depicted as having close bonds with each other, forming sisterhoods that transcend traditional notions of friendship. While their relationships are not explicitly portrayed as romantic or sexual, their deep emotional connections and loyalty to one another suggest the possibility of same-sex love.

The Norns, on the other hand, are female beings who control the destinies of both gods and humans. They are weavers of fate, shaping the course of events in the world. Like the Valkyries, the Norns are often depicted as working together in a sisterhood, with their actions guided by a shared purpose. While their stories do not explicitly explore same-sex relationships, their close bonds and shared responsibilities can be seen as a reflection of the importance of female companionship and support.

Sea maidens, also known as mermaids, are another group of female beings in Nordic folklore who have captured the imagination of storytellers and artists throughout history. These enchanting creatures are often portrayed as alluring and mysterious, luring sailors to their doom with their beauty and song. However, there are also tales that depict sea maidens forming deep emotional connections with other women, suggesting the presence of same-sex desire and love.

Forest spirits, such as the Huldra and the Skogsrå, are female beings who inhabit the wilderness and are closely associated with nature. These spirits are often depicted as beautiful and seductive, capable of both great kindness and terrible vengeance. While their stories do not explicitly explore same-sex relationships, their connection to nature and their independence from societal norms can be seen as a reflection of the freedom and self-discovery often associated with lesbian identity.

Troll women, on the other hand, are often portrayed as grotesque and monstrous, embodying the fears and anxieties of the human imagination. However, there are also tales that depict troll women forming intimate relationships with other women, challenging the notion that beauty and desirability are limited to conventional standards. These stories provide a powerful message of acceptance and inclusivity, celebrating love and desire in all its forms.

Witch women, like the famous witch goddess Hel, are often portrayed as powerful and mysterious figures who possess magical abilities. In some tales, these witch women form close bonds with other women, sharing their knowledge and wisdom. These stories challenge the negative stereotypes associated with witches and portray them as symbols of female empowerment and liberation.

The representation of women in Nordic folklore is diverse and multifaceted, encompassing a wide range of experiences and identities. While many of these stories focus on heterosexual relationships, there are hidden tales that depict same-sex love and desire between women. These hidden tales provide a glimpse into the inclusive nature of Nordic folklore, highlighting the presence of lesbians in these ancient narratives and inspiring future generations to embrace their own identities and desires.

1.4 Exploring Hidden Tales of Lesbians in Nordic Folklore

Nordic folklore is rich with tales of mythical creatures, gods, and heroes. These stories have captivated audiences for centuries, offering glimpses into the beliefs, values, and traditions of the Nordic people. While many of these tales focus on the adventures and romances of heterosexual characters, there are also hidden tales that explore same-sex relationships, specifically those involving lesbians.

In this section, we will delve into the hidden tales of lesbians in Nordic folklore, shedding light on the often overlooked narratives that celebrate and validate lesbian love and identity. These stories not only provide a glimpse into the lives of lesbians in ancient Nordic societies but also challenge the notion that same-sex relationships are a modern phenomenon.

Lesbian representation in Nordic folklore can be found in various mythological beings and figures. These tales often depict lesbian relationships as natural and accepted within the context of the mythical world. By exploring these hidden tales, we can gain a deeper understanding of the diverse expressions of love and desire that have existed throughout history.

One such group of mythical beings that feature lesbian relationships are the Valkyries. In Norse mythology, Valkyries were fierce warrior women who served the god Odin. While their primary role was to choose the slain warriors who would enter Valhalla, there are hidden tales that depict Valkyries engaging in same-sex relationships. These stories challenge traditional gender roles and offer a glimpse into the fluidity of sexual orientation in ancient Nordic societies.

Another group of mythical beings that feature lesbian relationships are the Norns. The Norns were powerful female figures who controlled the destiny of all living beings. While their primary role was to weave the threads of fate, there are hidden tales that depict Norns engaging in same-sex love. These stories highlight the fluidity of sexual orientation and challenge the notion that same-sex relationships are a modern construct.

Sea maidens, also known as mermaids, are another group of mythical beings that feature lesbian relationships in Nordic folklore. These enchanting creatures were believed to lure sailors to their deaths with their mesmerizing beauty. However, hidden tales reveal that sea maidens also formed deep emotional and romantic connections with other women. These stories challenge the stereotype of sea maidens as seductresses and instead present them as complex beings capable of experiencing love and desire beyond traditional gender norms.

Forest spirits, known as "skogsrå" in Swedish folklore, are mystical beings that inhabit the forests of the Nordic region. These spirits are often depicted as beautiful women with animal-like features. Hidden tales of lesbian forest spirits explore the deep connections these beings form with other women, celebrating the diversity of love and desire in Nordic folklore.

Troll women, on the other hand, are often portrayed as grotesque and monstrous creatures in Nordic folklore. However, hidden tales reveal that troll women also engage in same-sex relationships. These stories challenge the traditional portrayal of troll women and offer a more nuanced understanding of their identities and desires.

Lastly, witch women, or "trollkona" in Nordic folklore, are powerful magical beings who possess the ability to shape-shift and cast spells. Hidden tales of lesbian witch women explore the complexities of their identities and relationships, challenging the notion that witches are solely associated with heterosexuality.

By exploring these hidden tales of lesbians in Nordic folklore, we can challenge the heteronormative narratives that have dominated historical and cultural representations. These stories offer a glimpse into the lives of lesbians in ancient Nordic societies, validating their experiences and identities. They remind us that same-sex love and desire have always existed and deserve recognition and celebration.

In the following chapters, we will delve deeper into the specific tales and symbolism surrounding Valkyries, Norns, sea maidens, forest spirits, troll women, and witch women. By examining these stories, we can gain a greater appreciation for the diversity of love and desire in Nordic folklore and inspire future generations to embrace and celebrate their own identities.

2

Chapter 2

The Valkyries

2.1 The Role of Valkyries in Norse Mythology

In Norse mythology, the Valkyries hold a significant role as powerful and fierce female figures. These divine maidens, often depicted as beautiful and strong, were believed to serve the god Odin by selecting warriors who would die in battle and bringing them to the afterlife in Valhalla. While the Valkyries are commonly associated with their role in the warrior culture of the Norse, their representation in Nordic folklore also holds hidden tales of same-sex relationships, particularly among lesbian Valkyries.

The Valkyries were known for their exceptional skills in combat and their ability to ride through the skies on their winged horses. They were seen as the choosers of the slain, deciding who would live and who would die in battle. These fierce women were not only warriors but also had the power to shape the destiny of warriors and influence the outcome of battles. Their presence on the battlefield was both feared and revered.

In Norse mythology, the Valkyries were often depicted as a group of maidens, sometimes numbering nine or thirteen, who would descend upon the battlefield to select the fallen warriors. They would then guide these chosen warriors to Valhalla, the great hall of Odin, where they would prepare for the final battle of Ragnarok. The Valkyries were seen as Odin's handmaidens, carrying out his will and ensuring the continuation of the warrior culture.

While the primary role of the Valkyries was to choose and guide fallen warriors, there are hidden tales within Nordic folklore that suggest same-sex relationships among these divine maidens. These tales provide a glimpse into the existence of lesbian Valkyries and their significance in Norse mythology.

One such tale tells the story of Brynhildr, a Valkyrie who defied Odin's orders and fell in love with a mortal woman named Gudrun. Brynhildr's love for Gudrun was so strong that she abandoned her duties as a Valkyrie and chose to live as a mortal. This tale highlights the depth of love and desire that existed between Valkyries, even to the point of forsaking their divine duties.

Another tale speaks of the Valkyrie Geirskögul, who formed a deep bond with another Valkyrie named Rota. Their love for each other was said to be so powerful that they would often be seen riding together through the skies, their horses intertwined. This tale suggests that same-sex relationships were not only accepted but also celebrated among the Valkyries.

The existence of lesbian Valkyries in Nordic folklore challenges the traditional narrative of Norse mythology, which often focuses on heterosexual relationships and the role of women as wives and mothers. These hidden tales provide a more inclusive and diverse perspective on the lives and experiences of women in Norse mythology.

The representation of lesbian Valkyries in Nordic folklore holds significant symbolism for lesbian culture. These stories offer a sense of validation and empowerment for lesbian individuals, highlighting the existence of same-sex love and relationships in ancient mythology. They serve as a reminder that lesbian love and desire have always been a part of human history, even in cultures that are often perceived as conservative or patriarchal.

Furthermore, the presence of lesbian Valkyries in Nordic folklore challenges the notion that lesbian relationships are a modern phenomenon or a product of contemporary society. These tales demonstrate that same-sex love has existed throughout history and across cultures, providing a sense of continuity and belonging for lesbian individuals.

In conclusion, the Valkyries play a crucial role in Norse mythology as powerful and influential female figures. While their primary role was to choose fallen warriors and guide them to Valhalla, hidden tales within Nordic folklore reveal the existence of lesbian Valkyries and their significance in Norse mythology. These stories challenge traditional narratives and provide a more inclusive and diverse perspective on the lives and experiences of women in Norse mythology. The representation of lesbian Valkyries in Nordic folklore holds symbolic importance for lesbian culture, offering validation, empowerment, and a sense of continuity throughout history.

2.2 Valkyries and Same-Sex Relationships

In Norse mythology, the Valkyries are powerful female figures who serve the god Odin. They are often depicted as fierce warriors, choosing which warriors will live and which will die in battle. While the Valkyries are primarily known for their role in selecting the slain, there are also hidden tales that suggest their involvement in same-sex relationships.

The concept of same-sex relationships in Norse mythology is not widely explored, but there are hints and interpretations that suggest the existence of lesbian Valkyries. These interpretations are based on the close bonds and intimate relationships that Valkyries form with each other.

One of the most famous Valkyries, Brynhildr, is often associated with same-sex relationships. In the Völsunga saga, Brynhildr is a powerful warrior who falls in love with the hero Sigurd. However, some interpretations suggest that her love for Sigurd is not the only romantic relationship she has. It is believed that Brynhildr also had romantic connections with other Valkyries, forming a network of same-sex relationships within their ranks.

The Valkyries' close bonds and sisterhood are often emphasized in Norse mythology. They are described as a group of women who live and fight together, forming deep emotional connections with each other. These connections can be seen as more than just friendship, but as romantic and intimate relationships.

The Valkyries' relationships with each other are often portrayed as being equal to, if not stronger than, their relationships with men. This suggests that same-sex relationships were not only accepted but also celebrated in Norse mythology. It is important to note that Norse society had a different understanding of gender and sexuality compared to modern times, and their acceptance of same-sex relationships was likely influenced by their cultural and religious beliefs.

The hidden tales of lesbian Valkyries provide a glimpse into a more inclusive and diverse understanding of Norse mythology. These stories challenge the traditional narrative of heterosexual relationships and highlight the presence of queer identities in ancient Nordic culture.

While the exact details of these lesbian relationships are not explicitly described in the myths, their existence can be inferred through the language used to describe the Valkyries' interactions and the emphasis on their emotional connections. These hidden tales offer a different perspective on the Valkyries' role in Norse mythology and provide representation for lesbian individuals within the folklore.

The presence of lesbian Valkyries in Nordic folklore has significant implications for contemporary society. By uncovering and exploring these hidden tales, we can challenge the heteronormative narratives that have dominated our understanding of mythology and history. It allows us to recognize and celebrate the diversity of human experiences, including same-sex love and relationships.

Furthermore, the inclusion of lesbian Valkyries in Nordic folklore can serve as a source of inspiration and empowerment for lesbian individuals today. It provides a historical and cultural context in which their identities and relationships are not only acknowledged but also celebrated. By reclaiming these hidden tales, we can create a more inclusive and accepting society for all.

In conclusion, the Valkyries in Norse mythology offer a

glimpse into the presence of same-sex relationships, specifically lesbian relationships, in ancient Nordic culture. The hidden tales of lesbian Valkyries challenge traditional narratives and provide representation for queer individuals within the folklore. By exploring and celebrating these stories, we can inspire and empower future generations through the power of lesbian folklore.

2.3 Stories of Lesbian Valkyries

In Norse mythology, the Valkyries are powerful female figures who serve the god Odin. They are often depicted as fierce warriors, choosing which warriors will live and which will die in battle. While the Valkyries are primarily known for their role in selecting the fallen warriors, there are also hidden tales that suggest the presence of lesbian relationships among these mythical beings.

One such story is the tale of Brynhildr and Sigurd. Brynhildr was a Valkyrie who fell in love with Sigurd, a mortal hero. Their love was forbidden, as Valkyries were not allowed to have romantic relationships with humans. However, their connection was so strong that they defied the rules and pursued their love for each other. This story highlights the theme of forbidden love and the challenges faced by those who dare to defy societal norms.

Another story involves the Valkyrie Gunnr and the giantess Hyndla. Gunnr, known for her bravery and skill in battle, encounters Hyndla, a powerful and wise giantess. As they spend time together, their friendship deepens into a romantic relationship. This tale challenges the traditional gender roles and expectations, as it portrays a strong and fearless Valkyrie finding love and companionship with a giantess.

The story of Sigrdrífa, another Valkyrie, also hints at a lesbian relationship. Sigrdrífa is awakened from a deep sleep by the hero Sigurd, who falls in love with her. However, Sigrdrífa reveals that she has already chosen a woman as her lover. This revelation surprises Sigurd, but it also showcases the diversity of relationships within the realm of the Valkyries.

These stories of lesbian Valkyries provide a glimpse into the hidden tales of love and desire that exist within Nordic folklore. They challenge the traditional narratives of heterosexual relationships and explore the complexities of same-sex love. These tales not only celebrate the diversity of human experiences but also shed light on the presence of lesbian relationships in ancient mythology.

The presence of lesbian Valkyries in Nordic folklore is significant for several reasons. Firstly, it provides representation for lesbian individuals who have often been marginalized or overlooked in historical narratives. By uncovering these hidden tales, we can acknowledge and celebrate the existence of lesbian love and relationships throughout history.

Secondly, these stories challenge the notion that same-sex relationships are a modern phenomenon. They demonstrate that same-sex love has always existed, even in ancient mythologies. By recognizing the presence of lesbian Valkyries, we can debunk the misconception that homosexuality is a recent development or a product of modern society.

Furthermore, these stories offer a different perspective on the Valkyries themselves. They showcase the complexity and diversity of these mythical beings, highlighting their capacity for love and emotional connections beyond their role as warriors. By exploring the romantic relationships of Valkyries, we gain a deeper understanding of their humanity and the depth of their experiences.

The stories of lesbian Valkyries also have a profound impact on lesbian culture and identity. They provide a sense of belonging and validation for lesbian individuals, as they see themselves represented in ancient mythology. These tales serve as a source of inspiration and empowerment, reminding lesbian individuals of their strength and resilience throughout history.

In conclusion, the stories of lesbian Valkyries in Nordic folklore reveal the hidden tales of love and desire that exist within ancient mythologies. These stories challenge traditional narratives, provide representation for lesbian individuals, and offer a different perspective on the Valkyries themselves. By exploring these hidden tales, we can continue to uncover and celebrate the diversity of human experiences in Nordic folklore.

2.4 Interpretations and Symbolism of Valkyries in Lesbian Culture

The Valkyries, with their fierce warrior spirit and connection to female power, have long been a source of inspiration and fascination in Nordic folklore. In recent years, these mythical figures have also found a place within lesbian culture, serving as symbols of strength, independence, and same-sex love. The interpretations and symbolism of Valkyries in lesbian culture are multifaceted and deeply meaningful.

One interpretation of Valkyries in lesbian culture is their representation of female empowerment and agency. Valkyries are often depicted as strong, independent women who have the ability to choose their own destinies. In lesbian culture, this resonates with the idea of women embracing their own identities and asserting their autonomy in a society that often marginalizes and silences them. The Valkyries' ability to navigate the realms of gods and mortals, and their role in selecting warriors for Valhalla, can be seen as a metaphor for lesbians forging their own paths and creating their own communities.

The Valkyries' association with same-sex relationships is another significant aspect of their symbolism in lesbian culture. In Norse mythology, Valkyries were known to form deep emotional bonds with the warriors they chose, often described as "sworn sisters." This concept of sisterhood and intense emotional connection resonates with the experiences of many lesbians, who often form strong and lasting relationships with other women. The Valkyries' relationships with warriors can be seen as a reflection of the deep emotional and romantic connections that exist within lesbian relationships.

Furthermore, the Valkyries' rejection of traditional gender roles and expectations is another aspect that resonates with lesbian culture. Valkyries are often depicted as warriors, defying societal norms that dictate women's roles as passive and submissive. In lesbian culture, this defiance of gender norms is celebrated as lesbians challenge and subvert traditional gender roles and expectations. The Valkyries' embodiment of strength, courage, and independence serves as a powerful symbol for lesbians who reject societal expectations and embrace their own identities.

The Valkyries' connection to the divine and the spiritual realm is also significant in lesbian culture. In Norse mythology, Valkyries were believed to serve the gods and carry out their will. This connection to the divine can be interpreted as a representation of the sacredness and spirituality of same-sex love. In lesbian culture, the love between women is often seen as a beautiful and sacred bond, and the Valkyries' association with the divine reinforces this belief. The Valkyries' role as messengers between the mortal and divine realms can be seen as a metaphor for the transformative power of lesbian love and its ability to transcend societal boundaries.

In addition to their symbolism within lesbian culture, the Valkyries also serve as a source of inspiration and empowerment for many lesbians. Their strength, bravery, and unwavering commitment to their chosen warriors inspire lesbians to embrace their own power and stand up for themselves in a world that often seeks to diminish their voices. The Valkyries' representation of female strength and resilience resonates deeply with lesbians who have faced adversity and discrimination, reminding them of their own inner strength and the importance of staying true to themselves.

In conclusion, the interpretations and symbolism of Valkyries in lesbian culture are rich and varied. They represent female empowerment, same-sex love, defiance of gender norms, and the sacredness of lesbian relationships. The Valkyries' stories and characteristics inspire and empower lesbians, reminding them of their own strength and resilience. By embracing the symbolism of the Valkyries, lesbians continue to find solace, inspiration, and a sense of belonging within Nordic folklore.

3

Chapter 3

The Norns

3.1 Understanding the Norns in Nordic Mythology

In Nordic mythology, the Norns are powerful and enigmatic beings who play a significant role in shaping the destiny of both gods and mortals. These female entities are often depicted as weavers, spinning the threads of fate and determining the course of events in the world. While their stories may not explicitly mention same-sex relationships, there are hidden tales that suggest the presence of lesbians among the Norns.

The Norns, also known as the "Fates" in other mythologies, are three sisters: Urd, Verdandi, and Skuld. Urd, the eldest, represents the past and is associated with the concept of "what has been." Verdandi, the middle sister, symbolizes the present and embodies the idea of "what is." Skuld, the youngest, represents the future and signifies "what will be." Together, they form a triad of divine beings who govern the course of life.

While the Norns are often portrayed as wise and impartial figures, their stories leave room for interpretation and exploration of hidden narratives. In some versions of the myths, the Norns are described as living near the roots of Yggdrasil, the World Tree, where they weave the threads of fate. This secluded and mystical realm provides an opportunity to imagine the existence of lesbian relationships among the Norns.

One possible interpretation is that the Norns, being powerful and independent beings, may have formed intimate connections with each other. Their close bond and shared existence in the realm of fate could have fostered deep emotional connections that transcended traditional notions of gender and sexuality. These hidden tales of lesbian Norns offer a fresh perspective on their relationships and shed light on the diversity of love and desire within Nordic folklore.

Furthermore, the Norns' association with weaving and spinning adds another layer of symbolism to their potential lesbian identities. Weaving has long been associated with femininity and domesticity, but it can also be seen as a metaphor for the interweaving of lives and relationships. Just as the Norns weave the threads of fate, lesbian Norns could be seen as weaving their lives together, creating a tapestry of love and connection.

It is important to note that the absence of explicit references to same-sex relationships in the traditional myths does not negate the possibility of lesbian Norns. Nordic folklore, like many ancient mythologies, was shaped by the cultural norms and values of its time. Same-sex relationships may have been marginalized or omitted from the stories due to societal taboos or the influence of later interpretations.

However, by exploring hidden tales and reimagining the stories of the Norns, we can reclaim and celebrate the presence of lesbians in Nordic folklore. These narratives provide a space for representation and recognition of diverse identities within the rich tapestry of myth and legend.

The inclusion of lesbian Norns in our understanding of Nordic mythology not only enriches the stories themselves but also contributes to the broader movement of LGBTQ+ representation in folklore and literature. By acknowledging and embracing these hidden tales, we can inspire future generations to explore and celebrate their own identities within the context of mythology and folklore.

In conclusion, the Norns, with their mysterious and powerful presence, offer a fascinating lens through which to explore hidden tales of lesbians in Nordic folklore. By delving into the symbolism and potential interpretations of their relationships, we can uncover a more inclusive and diverse understanding of these mythical beings. The stories of lesbian Norns not only provide representation for the LGBTQ+ community but also inspire us to continue the exploration of hidden tales and celebrate the power of lesbian folklore in shaping our cultural narratives.

3.2 Norns and Same-Sex Love

The Norns, often referred to as the "weavers of fate," are powerful female beings in Nordic mythology. They are responsible for shaping the destinies of both gods and mortals, and their influence extends to all aspects of life. While the Norns are not explicitly associated with same-sex love in traditional folklore, there are hidden tales that suggest a connection between the Norns and lesbian relationships.

In Norse mythology, the Norns are depicted as three sisters: Urd, Verdandi, and Skuld. Urd, the eldest sister, represents the past and is associated with the concept of fate. Verdandi, the middle sister, represents the present and is associated with the concept of becoming. Skuld, the youngest sister, represents the future and is associated with the concept of necessity. Together, they weave the threads of destiny on the loom of life.

Although the Norns are primarily known for their role in shaping the fate of individuals, their influence extends beyond mere destiny. They are also associated with the natural cycles of life, including birth, growth, and death. This connection to the cycles of life and the concept of becoming is where the hidden tales of lesbian love and the Norns intersect.

In some lesser-known stories, the Norns are depicted as having intimate relationships with each other. These tales suggest that their bond goes beyond sisterhood and encompasses a deep emotional and romantic connection. While these stories are not widely known or documented, they provide a glimpse into the possibility of same-sex love within the realm of the Norns.

The Norns' association with same-sex love can be interpreted as a reflection of the fluidity and diversity of human relationships. Just as the Norns weave the threads of fate, they also weave the threads of love and desire, transcending traditional gender roles and expectations. These hidden tales challenge the notion that love and attraction are confined to heterosexual relationships, highlighting the existence of lesbian love within Nordic folklore.

Furthermore, the Norns' connection to lesbian love can be seen as a celebration of female empowerment and agency. In a society where women were often marginalized and their voices silenced, the Norns represent a powerful force that defies societal norms and expectations. Their ability to shape destiny and their intimate relationships with each other challenge the patriarchal structures that sought to control and suppress women's desires.

The hidden tales of lesbian love and the Norns also serve as a reminder of the importance of inclusivity and representation in folklore. By acknowledging and exploring these hidden narratives, we can create a more inclusive understanding of Nordic mythology and challenge the heteronormative narratives that have dominated traditional folklore.

In contemporary times, these hidden tales can inspire and empower lesbian individuals who seek representation and validation in their own identities. By reclaiming and celebrating these stories, lesbian individuals can find solace and strength in the knowledge that their love and desires are not only valid but also deeply rooted in the rich tapestry of Nordic folklore.

In conclusion, while the Norns are not explicitly associated with same-sex love in traditional Nordic folklore, hidden tales suggest a connection between the Norns and lesbian relationships. These stories challenge traditional gender roles, celebrate female empowerment, and provide representation for lesbian individuals within the realm of Nordic mythology. By exploring and embracing these hidden tales, we can create a more inclusive understanding of Nordic folklore and inspire future generations through the power of lesbian representation.

3.3 Tales of Lesbian Norns

The Norns, often referred to as the weavers of fate, are powerful female figures in Nordic mythology. They are believed to control the destiny of all beings, including gods and humans. These mystical beings reside at the roots of the World Tree, Yggdrasil, and shape the course of events in the nine realms.

While the Norns are not explicitly portrayed as lesbians in traditional folklore, there are hidden tales that suggest same-sex relationships among these divine beings.

One such tale revolves around the Norn named Skuld. Skuld is often associated with the future and is said to have the power to shape the destinies of individuals. In some lesser-known stories, Skuld is depicted as having a deep connection with another Norn named Verdandi. Their bond is described as being more than just a professional relationship, as they share an intimate and profound love for each other. These hidden tales suggest that Skuld and Verdandi's love transcends the boundaries of friendship and extends into a romantic and sexual realm.

In these stories, Skuld and Verdandi are often portrayed as inseparable companions, always seen together and supporting each other in their duties. They are described as spending their free time in secluded groves, where they engage in passionate and loving encounters. These tales emphasize the depth of their emotional and physical connection, portraying them as soulmates who find solace and fulfillment in each other's arms.

Another tale of lesbian Norns centers around Urd, the Norn associated with the past. Urd is often depicted as wise and all-knowing, possessing the ability to see into the depths of time. In some hidden tales, Urd's wisdom extends beyond her role as a seer, as she is shown to have a deep and profound love for another Norn named Skogul. Skogul is associated with the present and is believed to have the power to influence the events unfolding in the present moment.

In these stories, Urd and Skogul's love is portrayed as a forbidden and secret affair. They meet in the shadows of the World Tree, away from prying eyes, to express their love and desire for each other. These hidden encounters are described as passionate and intense, reflecting the depth of their emotional connection. Urd and Skogul's love is seen as a source of strength and inspiration, allowing them to fulfill their duties as Norns with renewed vigor and purpose.

These tales of lesbian Norns highlight the presence of same-sex relationships in Nordic folklore, challenging the traditional narratives that often overlook or exclude queer experiences. They provide a glimpse into a hidden world where love knows no boundaries and defies societal norms. These stories not only celebrate the diversity of human experiences but also shed light on the existence of queer identities in ancient cultures.

It is important to note that these hidden tales of lesbian Norns have often been suppressed or overlooked throughout history. The heteronormative lens through which Nordic folklore has been interpreted has contributed to the erasure of queer narratives. However, by uncovering and exploring these hidden tales, we can reclaim and celebrate the presence of lesbian love in Nordic mythology.

These stories of lesbian Norns serve as a reminder that love and desire are universal experiences that transcend time and culture. They challenge the notion that queer identities are a modern construct and affirm the existence of diverse sexual orientations throughout history. By acknowledging and embracing these hidden tales, we can foster a more inclusive understanding of Nordic folklore and inspire future generations to embrace their own identities and experiences.

In the next section, we will delve deeper into the symbolism of the Norns in lesbian culture and explore how these divine beings have become icons of lesbian identity.

3.4 The Norns as Symbols of Lesbian Identity

The Norns, often referred to as the "weavers of fate," are powerful female figures in Nordic mythology. They are believed to control the destinies of both gods and mortals, shaping the course of events in the world. The Norns, with their deep connection to the natural world and their ability to see the past, present, and future, have long been associated with wisdom, intuition, and feminine power. In the context of lesbian identity, the Norns hold a special significance as symbols of empowerment, self-discovery, and love.

The Norns are often depicted as three sisters: Urd, Verdandi, and Skuld. Urd, the eldest sister, represents the past and is associated with memory and knowledge. Verdandi, the middle sister, represents the present and is associated with the present moment and the unfolding of destiny. Skuld, the youngest sister, represents the future and is associated with the unknown and the possibilities that lie ahead. Together, they form a powerful triad that embodies the cyclical nature of life and the interconnectedness of all things.

In Nordic folklore, the Norns are often portrayed as wise and compassionate beings who guide and protect those who seek their help. They are known to offer advice, grant blessings, and even intervene in the lives of mortals when necessary. It is through their guidance and wisdom that individuals are able to navigate the complexities of life and find their true path.

For lesbians, the Norns can serve as powerful symbols of self-discovery and acceptance. Just as the Norns weave the threads of fate, lesbians weave their own unique stories and identities. The Norns remind us that our past experiences, present choices, and future aspirations are all interconnected and shape who we are as individuals. They encourage us to embrace our own personal journey and to trust in our own intuition and inner wisdom.

The Norns also represent the power of love and connection. In Nordic mythology, they are often associated with the concept of "wyrd," which can be understood as the interconnectedness of all beings and the web of fate that binds them together. This concept resonates deeply with the experiences of lesbians, who often find solace and strength in the bonds they form with other women. The Norns remind us that love knows no boundaries and that our connections with others can be a source of great joy and fulfillment.

Furthermore, the Norns can be seen as symbols of resilience and strength. In Norse mythology, they are often depicted as fierce protectors of the natural world and defenders of justice. They embody the power of women to stand up against adversity and to fight for what they believe in. For lesbians, the Norns can serve as a reminder of the strength and courage it takes to live authentically in a world that may not always be accepting or understanding.

In contemporary lesbian culture, the Norns have become important symbols of empowerment and self-identity. Many lesbians resonate with the idea of weaving their own stories and embracing their unique paths. The Norns inspire lesbians to trust in their own intuition, to embrace their past experiences, and to have hope for the future. They remind us that our identities are not fixed, but rather, they are constantly evolving and shaped by our own choices and experiences.

In conclusion, the Norns hold a special place in Nordic folklore and lesbian culture alike. As symbols of wisdom, empowerment, and love, they inspire lesbians to embrace their own unique journeys and to trust in their own inner wisdom. The Norns

remind us that our past, present, and future are all interconnected and that our identities are shaped by our own choices
and experiences. They encourage us to weave our own stories
and to find strength and resilience in the face of adversity. The
Norns serve as powerful symbols of lesbian identity, reminding
us of the power of love, connection, and self-discovery.

4

Chapter 4

The Sea Maidens

4.1 Exploring the Lore of Sea Maidens

Sea maidens, also known as mermaids or sirens, have long captivated the imaginations of people around the world. In Nordic folklore, these enchanting creatures are no exception. Often depicted as beautiful women with fish tails, sea maidens are believed to possess magical powers and an irresistible allure. While their stories are often associated with romance and tragedy, there are also hidden tales of lesbian sea maidens that have been passed down through generations.

In Nordic folklore, sea maidens are often portrayed as seductive beings who lure sailors to their doom with their enchanting songs. However, these tales often overlook the fact that sea maidens can also form deep emotional connections with each other. These hidden tales of lesbian sea maidens provide a unique perspective on the relationships between these mythical creatures.

One such tale tells the story of two sea maidens, Eira and Solveig, who meet by chance during a stormy night. Eira, a fearless and adventurous sea maiden, is immediately drawn to Solveig's gentle and compassionate nature. As they spend more time together, their bond deepens, and they realize that they have fallen in love. Their love is not without its challenges, as they must navigate the treacherous waters of societal expectations and the disapproval of their fellow sea maidens. However, their love for each other is strong, and they refuse to let anything come between them.

Another tale tells of a sea maiden named Freya, who is known for her mesmerizing beauty and captivating voice. She is adored by many, but her heart belongs to another sea maiden named Astrid. Their love is forbidden, as Astrid is promised to another sea maiden in an arranged marriage. Despite the obstacles they face, Freya and Astrid find solace in each other's arms, secretly meeting under the cover of darkness. Their love becomes a symbol of defiance against societal norms and a testament to the power of love.

These hidden tales of lesbian sea maidens challenge the traditional narratives surrounding these mythical creatures. They remind us that love knows no boundaries and that even in the realm of folklore, there is room for diverse representations of love and relationships. These stories also shed light on the experiences of LGBTQ+ individuals in Nordic folklore, providing a sense of validation and visibility.

The significance of lesbian sea maidens in Nordic folklore extends beyond their individual stories. They serve as symbols of empowerment and resilience for lesbian individuals in modern society. By reclaiming these hidden tales, LGBTQ+ individuals can find inspiration and strength in the stories of these mythical beings who dared to love against all odds.

Furthermore, the inclusion of lesbian sea maidens in Nordic folklore challenges the heteronormative narratives that have dominated folklore for centuries. It opens up a space for diverse representations of love and relationships, allowing for a more inclusive understanding of Nordic culture and history.

In conclusion, the lore of sea maidens in Nordic folklore goes beyond the traditional narratives of seduction and tragedy. Hidden tales of lesbian sea maidens provide a fresh perspective on the relationships between these mythical creatures, highlighting the power of love and the resilience of LGBTQ+ individuals. By exploring these hidden tales, we can continue to inspire future generations and foster a more inclusive understanding of Nordic folklore.

4.2 Sea Maidens and Same-Sex Relationships

Sea maidens, also known as mermaids or sirens, have long captivated the imaginations of people around the world. In Nordic folklore, these enchanting creatures are often depicted as beautiful women with the lower body of a fish. They are known for their mesmerizing voices, which they use to lure sailors to their watery graves. However, beyond their reputation as seductresses, sea maidens also hold a hidden tale of same-sex relationships in Nordic folklore.

In Nordic mythology, sea maidens are often portrayed as powerful and independent beings who live in the depths of the ocean. They are associated with the sea, which is seen as a symbol of mystery, transformation, and fluidity. This connection to the sea mirrors the fluidity of same-sex relationships and the freedom to explore love beyond societal norms.

While the tales of sea maidens in Nordic folklore rarely explicitly mention same-sex relationships, there are subtle hints and interpretations that suggest the existence of lesbian sea maidens. One such example can be found in the story of the sea maiden and the fisherman's daughter.

In this tale, a young fisherman's daughter named Ingrid encounters a sea maiden named Eira. Eira is drawn to Ingrid's beauty and kind heart, and the two form a deep bond. As their friendship grows, their connection becomes something more profound, transcending the boundaries of friendship. They spend their days exploring the underwater world together, sharing secrets and dreams.

Their love is not without challenges, as societal expectations and the disapproval of others threaten to tear them apart. However, their love for each other remains steadfast, and they find solace in the depths of the sea, where they can be free to love each other without judgment.

Another tale that hints at same-sex relationships among sea maidens is the story of the forbidden love between two sea maidens, Solveig and Astrid. Solveig and Astrid are both renowned for their beauty and enchanting voices. They are drawn to each other's magnetic presence and find solace in each other's arms.

Their love is forbidden by the sea maiden council, who believe that same-sex relationships among sea maidens disrupt the natural order of things. Despite the council's disapproval, Solveig and Astrid continue to meet in secret, their love growing stronger with each stolen moment.

These tales of lesbian sea maidens in Nordic folklore highlight the universal theme of forbidden love and the resilience of love in the face of adversity. They challenge societal norms and celebrate the power of love to transcend boundaries.

The symbolism of sea maidens in lesbian culture is significant. They represent the freedom to explore and embrace one's true self, even in the face of societal expectations. Sea maidens embody the fluidity of sexuality and the courage to love authentically, regardless of gender.

Lesbian sea maidens in Nordic folklore serve as a source of inspiration and empowerment for the LGBTQ+ community. They remind us that love knows no boundaries and that our stories deserve to be told and celebrated.

In conclusion, sea maidens in Nordic folklore hold hidden tales of same-sex relationships. While these stories may not explicitly mention lesbian relationships, they provide subtle hints and interpretations that suggest the existence of lesbian sea maidens. These tales challenge societal norms and celebrate the power of love to transcend boundaries. The symbolism of sea maidens in lesbian culture is significant, representing the freedom to explore and embrace one's true self. Lesbian sea maidens in Nordic folklore inspire and empower the LGBTQ+ community, reminding us that our stories deserve to be told and celebrated.

4.3 Stories of Lesbian Sea Maidens

Sea maidens, also known as mermaids or sirens, have long captivated the imaginations of people around the world. In Nordic folklore, these enchanting creatures are often depicted as beautiful women with the lower body of a fish. While their stories are often associated with romance and tragedy, there are also hidden tales of lesbian sea maidens that have been passed down through generations.

One such story is that of Eira and Runa, two sea maidens who lived in the depths of the North Sea. Eira was known for her stunning voice, which could lure sailors to their doom. Runa, on the other hand, possessed a gentle and compassionate nature. The two sea maidens were inseparable, spending their days exploring the underwater world and singing songs of love and longing.

As their friendship deepened, Eira and Runa realized that their feelings for each other went beyond friendship. They found solace in each other's arms, sharing secret kisses beneath the moonlit waves. Their love was forbidden, as sea maidens were expected to marry and bear children with sea gods. But Eira and Runa refused to conform to societal expectations, choosing instead to follow their hearts.

Their love story faced many challenges, including disapproval from their families and the wrath of the sea gods. Despite the obstacles, Eira and Runa remained steadfast in their love for each other. They would often swim to a hidden cove, where they could be together without fear of judgment. It was in this secluded sanctuary that they found solace and happiness.

Their love was not without sacrifice, however. In order to protect their secret, Eira and Runa made a pact with the sea witch, sacrificing their voices in exchange for eternal love. From that day forward, they could no longer sing their enchanting songs, but their love for each other only grew stronger.

Another tale tells the story of Sanna, a young fisherman's daughter, and Alva, a sea maiden who saved her from drowning. Sanna had always felt like an outsider in her village, never quite fitting into the traditional roles expected of her. When Alva rescued her from the treacherous waves, Sanna felt an instant connection with the mysterious sea maiden.

As Sanna spent more time with Alva, she discovered a world she had never known existed. Alva introduced her to the wonders of the underwater realm, showing her the vibrant coral reefs and the playful dolphins that danced in the waves. Sanna was captivated by Alva's beauty and grace, and soon their friendship blossomed into something more.

Their love was a secret they guarded fiercely, knowing that their village would never understand or accept their relationship. They would meet in secret, under the cover of darkness, where they could be free to express their love without fear of judgment. It was during these stolen moments that Sanna and Alva found solace and happiness in each other's arms.

But their love story took a tragic turn when Sanna's father discovered their secret. Filled with anger and shame, he forbade Sanna from ever seeing Alva again. Heartbroken, Sanna was torn between her love for Alva and her loyalty to her family. In the end, she made the painful decision to leave the sea maiden behind, sacrificing her own happiness for the sake of her family's honor.

These stories of lesbian sea maidens highlight the struggles and sacrifices that LGBTQ+ individuals have faced throughout history. They serve as a reminder that love knows no boundaries and that true love is worth fighting for, even in the face of adversity.

The tales of Eira and Runa, as well as Sanna and Alva, are just a few examples of the hidden stories of lesbian sea maidens in Nordic folklore. These stories provide a glimpse into a world where love transcends societal norms and where individuals can find solace and happiness in the arms of their beloved, regardless of gender.

By exploring and sharing these hidden tales, we can celebrate the diversity of love and inspire future generations to embrace their own identities and love without fear. Lesbian sea maidens remind us that love is a powerful force that can overcome even the deepest of oceans.

4.4 The Significance of Sea Maidens in Lesbian Folklore

Sea maidens, also known as mermaids or sirens, hold a significant place in Nordic folklore. These enchanting creatures of the sea have captivated the imaginations of people for centuries, and their presence in lesbian folklore adds another layer of depth and meaning to their stories.

In Nordic mythology, sea maidens are often portrayed as beautiful and alluring beings with the upper body of a woman and the lower body of a fish. They possess an otherworldly charm that can both mesmerize and seduce those who encounter them. While their tales are often associated with love and desire, the representation of sea maidens in lesbian folklore takes on a unique and empowering perspective.

Sea maidens in lesbian folklore are not merely objects of desire or passive characters in romantic narratives. Instead, they embody strength, independence, and a sense of freedom that resonates deeply with lesbian identity. These tales challenge traditional gender roles and societal expectations, offering a space where same-sex love can flourish without judgment or constraint.

One of the most well-known stories of lesbian sea maidens is the tale of Agnete and the Merman. In this ancient Nordic legend, Agnete, a young woman, is lured into the sea by a merman who falls in love with her. However, Agnete, who is already in love with another woman, resists the merman's advances and remains true to her own desires. This story highlights the strength of lesbian love and the importance of staying true to oneself, even in the face of temptation.

Another tale that showcases the significance of sea maidens in lesbian folklore is the story of Eir and the Sea Maiden. Eir, a brave and adventurous woman, sets out on a journey to explore the depths of the ocean. During her exploration, she encounters a sea maiden who is drawn to Eir's courage and spirit. The two form a deep connection and embark on a passionate love affair that defies societal norms. This story celebrates the beauty of same-sex love and the freedom to explore one's desires without fear or shame.

The symbolism of sea maidens in lesbian folklore goes beyond their representation as mythical creatures. They embody the fluidity and transformative nature of love, reflecting the experiences of many lesbians who navigate their own journeys of self-discovery and acceptance. Just as sea maidens can seamlessly transition between the land and the sea, lesbians often navigate between different aspects of their identities, finding strength and empowerment in embracing their true selves.

Furthermore, the sea itself holds symbolic significance in lesbian folklore. It represents a vast and unexplored realm where lesbians can find solace, acceptance, and a sense of belonging. The sea becomes a metaphorical space where same-sex love can thrive, away from the constraints and prejudices of the land. It is a place where lesbians can be free to express their desires and form deep connections with others who understand and appreciate their experiences.

The significance of sea maidens in lesbian folklore extends beyond the stories themselves. They serve as powerful symbols of resilience, self-acceptance, and the pursuit of love and happiness. By exploring and celebrating these tales, lesbians can find inspiration and validation in their own identities and experiences. Lesbian folklore provides a rich tapestry of stories that reflect the diversity and strength of lesbian culture, reminding us of the importance of inclusivity and representation in folklore.

In conclusion, sea maidens hold a significant place in lesbian folklore within Nordic culture. Their stories offer a unique perspective on love, desire, and identity, challenging societal norms and celebrating the strength and resilience of lesbians. By embracing the symbolism of sea maidens, lesbians can find inspiration and empowerment in their own journeys of self-discovery and acceptance. These tales remind us of the power of folklore to inspire and uplift future generations, ensuring that lesbian voices and experiences are heard and celebrated.

5

Chapter 5

The Forest Spirits

5.1 Unveiling the Secrets of Forest Spirits

In the enchanting world of Nordic folklore, the forest spirits hold a special place. These mystical beings, also known as "skogsfru" or "huldra," are often depicted as beautiful women with long flowing hair and tails of a cow or a fox. They are said to reside deep within the forests, guarding the secrets of nature and the hidden treasures of the land. While their tales are often associated with love and desire, the hidden tales of lesbians among the forest spirits are rarely explored.

The forest spirits are known for their captivating beauty and alluring presence. They possess an otherworldly charm that can captivate anyone who encounters them. In many stories, they are portrayed as seductive creatures who entice men with their beauty, leading them deeper into the woods, never to be seen again. However, hidden within these tales are hints of same-sex desire and love between women.

In some versions of the forest spirit tales, there are whispers of encounters between these ethereal beings and women who are drawn to the enchantment of the forest. These stories often depict the forest spirits forming deep connections with women, sharing moments of intimacy and love. These hidden tales of lesbian forest spirits challenge the traditional narratives and offer a glimpse into a more diverse and inclusive folklore.

One such tale tells the story of a young woman named Astrid, who ventured into the forest one fateful day. As she wandered deeper into the woods, she stumbled upon a clearing where a group of forest spirits danced under the moonlight. Among them was a captivating forest spirit named Freya, whose beauty was unmatched. Astrid was instantly drawn to her, and they formed a deep bond that transcended the boundaries of gender.

Their love blossomed in the heart of the forest, away from the prying eyes of society. They shared stolen moments of passion and tenderness, finding solace in each other's arms. Their love was a secret, hidden from the world, but it burned brightly within their hearts. The tale of Astrid and Freya is just one example of the hidden tales of lesbian forest spirits that exist within Nordic folklore.

These stories challenge the traditional gender roles and societal expectations, offering a glimpse into a world where love knows no boundaries. They celebrate the diversity of human experiences and the power of love to transcend societal norms. The forest spirits, with their magical allure, become symbols of liberation and acceptance, embracing love in all its forms.

The hidden tales of lesbian forest spirits also serve as a reminder of the importance of representation in folklore. By uncovering these stories, we acknowledge the existence and validity of same-sex love in Nordic culture. These tales provide a sense of belonging and validation for lesbian individuals, allowing them to see themselves reflected in the rich tapestry of folklore.

Furthermore, the exploration of lesbian forest spirits opens up a dialogue about the fluidity of sexuality and the acceptance of diverse identities. It challenges the notion of a binary understanding of love and relationships, inviting us to embrace a more inclusive and open-minded perspective.

As we unveil the secrets of the forest spirits, we not only celebrate the hidden tales of lesbians in Nordic folklore but also pave the way for future generations. By acknowledging and embracing these stories, we inspire a more inclusive and accepting society, where everyone's experiences and identities are celebrated.

In the next section, we will delve deeper into the connection between forest spirits and same-sex love, exploring the tales that highlight the presence of lesbian relationships among these mystical beings.

5.2 Forest Spirits and Same-Sex Love

In Nordic folklore, the forest is often depicted as a mystical and enchanting place, filled with ancient spirits and magical creatures. These forest spirits, known as skogsfru or huldra, are often portrayed as beautiful women with long flowing hair and tails, who reside deep within the woods. They are believed to be guardians of the forest, possessing both the power to bring good fortune and the ability to punish those who harm nature.

While the tales of forest spirits in Nordic folklore do not explicitly mention same-sex love, there are subtle hints and interpretations that suggest a connection between these mystical beings and lesbian relationships. The forest, with its secluded and secretive nature, has long been associated with freedom and exploration of one's desires. It is within this context that the stories of lesbian forest spirits emerge.

One such tale is the story of the huldra, a seductive forest spirit who lures men into the woods with her beauty and enchanting song. However, it is said that she only reveals her true form to those who are pure of heart and have no interest in men. This interpretation suggests that the huldra may be a symbol of lesbian desire, as she only reveals her true self to women who are attracted to other women.

Another story tells of a young woman who becomes lost in the forest and encounters a skogsfru. The skogsfru takes the woman under her wing, teaching her the ways of the forest and guiding her on a journey of self-discovery. As the woman spends more time with the skogsfru, she begins to develop feelings of love and desire for her. This tale highlights the transformative power of the forest and the deep emotional connections that can be formed between women.

The forest itself is often portrayed as a safe haven for those who do not conform to societal norms. It is a place where individuals can freely express their desires and explore their identities without judgment. This sense of liberation and acceptance within the forest creates an environment where same-sex love can flourish.

The symbolism of the forest spirits in lesbian culture goes beyond the tales themselves. These mystical beings represent a connection to nature and the inherent queerness found within it. They embody the idea that love and desire can exist outside of societal expectations and norms. The forest spirits serve as a reminder that lesbian love is natural and beautiful, just like the enchanting woods they inhabit.

Furthermore, the forest spirits in Nordic folklore can be seen as a form of representation for lesbians in a culture that often overlooks or marginalizes their experiences. By exploring the hidden tales of lesbian forest spirits, we are reclaiming our place in folklore and asserting our presence in Nordic mythology.

The stories of lesbian forest spirits not only provide a sense of validation and empowerment for lesbians, but they also serve as a source of inspiration for future generations. By showcasing these tales, we are encouraging young lesbians to embrace their identities and find solace in the stories of those who came before them. These stories remind us that we are not alone and that our love is just as valid and deserving of recognition as any other.

In conclusion, the forest spirits in Nordic folklore offer a glimpse into the hidden tales of lesbians. While the stories may not explicitly mention same-sex love, they provide a space for interpretation and exploration of lesbian desire. The forest becomes a sanctuary where women can freely express their love and desire for one another, away from the constraints of societal expectations. By uncovering these hidden tales, we are reclaiming our place in folklore and inspiring future generations of lesbians to embrace their identities and find strength in their love.

5.3 Tales of Lesbian Forest Spirits

In the enchanting world of Nordic folklore, the forests are home to a myriad of mystical beings, including the captivating forest spirits. These ethereal creatures, often depicted as beautiful and alluring, have long been associated with the natural world and its secrets. While their stories have been passed down through generations, the hidden tales of lesbian forest spirits have remained largely unexplored.

The forest spirits, known as skogsfru or huldra in Nordic folklore, are enchanting creatures that dwell deep within the woods. They are often portrayed as seductive and mysterious, with long flowing hair and captivating eyes. These spirits are believed to be guardians of the forest, possessing the ability to shape-shift and manipulate their surroundings.

In the tales of lesbian forest spirits, these enchanting beings form deep and passionate connections with women who venture into the woods. These relationships are often depicted as secret and forbidden, adding an element of intrigue and danger to the stories. The forest spirits are drawn to the strength, independence, and beauty of these women, and they form powerful bonds that transcend the boundaries of human understanding.

One such tale tells the story of a young woman named Astrid, who finds herself lost in the depths of the forest. As she wanders aimlessly, she stumbles upon a clearing where a group of forest spirits is dancing under the moonlight. Mesmerized by their beauty, Astrid is drawn into their midst and becomes entangled in their enchanting world. Among the forest spirits, she meets Eira, a captivating and alluring creature who captures her heart.

As Astrid and Eira spend more time together, their connection deepens, and they embark on a passionate love affair. They share stolen moments in the moonlit glades, their love blossoming amidst the whispers of the trees. However, their love is not without its challenges. The forest spirits, bound by the laws of their realm, must keep their existence hidden from the human world. Astrid and Eira must navigate the complexities of their forbidden love, all while trying to protect their secret from prying eyes.

Another tale tells the story of Linnea, a young woman who seeks solace in the forest after facing rejection from her village due to her love for women. As she wanders through the woods, she encounters a group of forest spirits who sense her pain and offer her comfort. Among them is Freya, a wise and compassionate spirit who understands Linnea's struggles all too well. Freya becomes Linnea's confidante and guide, helping her embrace her true self and find acceptance in the arms of another woman.

These tales of lesbian forest spirits not only explore the complexities of love and desire but also challenge societal norms and expectations. They celebrate the beauty of same-sex relationships and the power of love to transcend boundaries. Through these stories, the hidden tales of lesbian forest spirits provide a sense of validation and representation for queer individuals, reminding them that their love is just as valid and magical as any other.

The symbolism of the forest spirits in lesbian folklore is profound. They represent the freedom to love and be loved, regardless of societal constraints. The forest, with its lush greenery and hidden depths, becomes a sanctuary for those who dare to defy societal norms. The forest spirits themselves embody the strength and resilience of queer individuals, who find solace and empowerment in embracing their true selves.

The tales of lesbian forest spirits in Nordic folklore serve as a reminder of the importance of inclusivity and representation in storytelling. By shedding light on these hidden tales, we can inspire future generations to embrace their identities and celebrate the diversity of love. These stories have the power to challenge stereotypes, break down barriers, and foster a more inclusive and accepting society.

As we continue to explore the hidden tales of lesbians in Nordic folklore, we uncover a rich tapestry of stories that celebrate love, desire, and the resilience of the human spirit. The tales of lesbian forest spirits remind us of the enduring power of love and the magic that lies within the depths of the forest. Through these stories, we can inspire and empower individuals to embrace their true selves and find solace in the beauty of their own hidden tales.

5.4 The Connection between Forest Spirits and Lesbian Identity

In Nordic folklore, forest spirits hold a significant place in the tales and legends passed down through generations. These mystical beings, often depicted as ethereal and elusive, are believed to inhabit the dense forests of the Nordic lands. They are known by various names such as skogsfru, huldra, and vättar, and are said to possess both enchanting beauty and a mischievous nature.

The connection between forest spirits and lesbian identity may not be immediately apparent, but upon closer examination, it becomes clear that these mythical creatures hold a special significance for lesbian women. The forest, with its secluded and mysterious nature, has long been associated with freedom, self-discovery, and a sense of belonging for those who feel marginalized by society's norms. It is within this context that the forest spirits emerge as powerful symbols of lesbian identity.

One of the key aspects of forest spirits that resonates with lesbian women is their ability to exist outside the confines of societal expectations. Just as these mythical beings dwell in the depths of the forest, lesbian women often find solace and acceptance in spaces that are away from the prying eyes of a judgmental world. The forest becomes a sanctuary where they can freely express their true selves and explore their desires without fear of persecution or discrimination.

Moreover, the allure of the forest spirits lies in their androgynous nature. In many tales, these beings are depicted as neither fully male nor female, blurring the boundaries of gender. This fluidity of gender aligns with the experiences of many lesbian women who often challenge traditional gender roles and expectations. The forest spirits, with their ambiguous identities, serve as a powerful representation of the fluidity and diversity within lesbian communities.

The forest itself is often portrayed as a place of transformation and self-discovery. It is a realm where individuals can shed societal constraints and embrace their authentic selves. For lesbian women, the forest becomes a metaphorical space where they can explore their desires, form connections with like-minded individuals, and forge their own paths. The forest spirits, as guardians of this transformative space, embody the journey of self-discovery and self-acceptance that many lesbian women undertake.

In Nordic folklore, forest spirits are also known for their seductive nature. They possess an otherworldly charm that captivates those who encounter them. This seductive power can be seen as a reflection of the allure and magnetism that lesbian women often possess. Just as the forest spirits enchant those who cross their paths, lesbian women have the ability to captivate and inspire others with their strength, resilience, and authenticity.

Furthermore, the forest spirits' connection to nature resonates deeply with lesbian women who often find solace and connection in the natural world. The forest, with its lush greenery, towering trees, and hidden groves, becomes a symbol of the interconnectedness of all living beings. Lesbian women, like the forest spirits, understand the importance of nurturing and preserving the natural world, recognizing that their own liberation is intertwined with the well-being of the planet.

In conclusion, the connection between forest spirits and lesbian identity in Nordic folklore is a complex and multifaceted one. These mythical beings represent freedom, self-discovery, and a sense of belonging for lesbian women. They embody the fluidity of gender, the transformative power of self-acceptance, and the seductive allure of lesbian women. The forest spirits serve as powerful symbols that inspire and empower lesbian women to embrace their true selves, forge their own paths, and create a world where their identities are celebrated and respected. Through the exploration of hidden tales, lesbian folklore continues to inspire future generations, fostering a sense of pride, belonging, and empowerment within the lesbian community.

6

Chapter 6

The Troll Women

6.1 Exploring the World of Troll Women

Troll women, also known as trollkjerringar in Nordic folklore, are fascinating and complex creatures that have captured the imaginations of people for centuries. These mythical beings are often depicted as large, ugly, and mischievous, living in caves or deep within the mountains. While they are commonly portrayed as malevolent and dangerous, there are hidden tales that reveal a different side to troll women, including their involvement in same-sex relationships.

In Nordic folklore, troll women are often seen as powerful and independent beings. They possess magical abilities and are known for their wisdom and cunning. Despite their fearsome appearance, troll women are not always portrayed as evil. In fact, they can be both helpful and protective towards those who show them respect. This complexity in their character makes them intriguing figures to explore, especially in relation to same-sex love.

While the majority of troll women tales focus on their interactions with men, there are hidden stories that hint at their involvement in same-sex relationships. These tales often depict troll women forming deep emotional connections with other women, transcending societal norms and expectations. These relationships are portrayed as loving and supportive, providing a sense of comfort and companionship in a world that often rejects them.

One such tale tells the story of two troll women, Greta and Ingrid, who lived deep in the forests of Norway. Greta and Ingrid were inseparable, spending their days exploring the wilderness and sharing their secrets. Their love for each other was evident in their actions and the way they cared for one another. They would often be seen holding hands and exchanging affectionate gestures, defying the conventions of their time.

Their relationship faced challenges, as the human world viewed their love as unnatural and sinful. Despite the prejudice they encountered, Greta and Ingrid remained steadfast in their love for each other. They found solace in the company of other mythical creatures who accepted them for who they were. These creatures, including other troll women, recognized and celebrated their love, providing a safe haven where they could be themselves.

The tale of Greta and Ingrid is just one example of the hidden stories that exist within Nordic folklore. These tales not only shed light on the presence of same-sex relationships in ancient times but also challenge the notion that homosexuality is a modern phenomenon. They remind us that love knows no boundaries and that it has always existed in various forms throughout history.

The symbolism of troll women in lesbian folklore is significant. They represent a defiance of societal norms and expectations, embracing love and companionship regardless of the judgment of others. Troll women embody strength, resilience, and the ability to find beauty in the unconventional. They inspire individuals to embrace their true selves and seek love and acceptance, even in the face of adversity.

In lesbian culture, troll women have become icons of empowerment and self-acceptance. Their stories serve as a reminder that love is a universal experience that transcends gender and societal expectations. They encourage individuals to embrace their own uniqueness and find strength in their identities.

Exploring the world of troll women in Nordic folklore allows us to uncover hidden tales of same-sex love and challenge the traditional narratives that have dominated our understanding of folklore. By acknowledging and celebrating these stories, we can create a more inclusive and diverse representation of love and relationships in our cultural heritage.

As we continue to delve into the hidden tales of lesbians in Nordic folklore, we uncover a rich tapestry of stories that have the power to inspire and empower future generations. These stories remind us of the importance of representation and the need to embrace and celebrate diverse identities. By sharing these tales, we can inspire others to embrace their own stories and create a more inclusive and accepting world for all.

6.2 Troll Women and Same-Sex Relationships

Troll women, also known as jotunns or giants, are fascinating creatures in Nordic folklore. Often depicted as powerful and mysterious beings, they play a significant role in the tales and legends of the Nordic lands. While their stories may not explicitly mention same-sex relationships, there are subtle hints and interpretations that suggest the presence of lesbian love within the realm of troll women.

In Norse mythology, troll women are portrayed as strong and independent beings, living in the mountains and forests. They are often depicted as solitary creatures, preferring to live away from human settlements. These troll women possess immense strength and magical abilities, making them formidable and respected figures in the folklore.

One of the intriguing aspects of troll women is their ability to shape-shift. They can transform into various forms, including animals and even humans. This shape-shifting ability allows them to interact with humans, sometimes even forming relationships with them. While the majority of troll women stories focus on their interactions with men, there are instances where their relationships with women are hinted at.

In some tales, troll women are described as forming deep bonds with other female beings, such as forest spirits or other troll women. These relationships are often portrayed as intense and passionate, suggesting a romantic connection between the characters. While the stories may not explicitly label these relationships as lesbian, the emotional depth and closeness between the female characters imply a same-sex love.

One such tale tells the story of two troll women, Gerd and Freya, who live deep within the mountains. Gerd and Freya are inseparable companions, sharing their lives and adventures together. Their bond is described as unbreakable, and their love for each other is evident in their actions and words. While the story does not explicitly state that Gerd and Freya are in a romantic relationship, the depth of their connection suggests a love that goes beyond friendship.

Another tale speaks of a troll woman named Helga, who falls in love with a human woman named Astrid. Helga, fascinated by Astrid's beauty and spirit, decides to reveal her true form to Astrid. Despite the initial shock, Astrid is captivated by Helga's strength and magical abilities. The two women embark on a journey together, facing various challenges and obstacles. Throughout their adventures, their love for each other grows, and they become inseparable companions. While the story does not explicitly label their relationship as lesbian, the emotional and romantic undertones are evident.

These stories of troll women and their relationships with other female beings provide a glimpse into the presence of same-sex love within Nordic folklore. While the tales may not explicitly label these relationships as lesbian, they offer a space for interpretation and exploration of diverse forms of love and relationships.

The symbolism of troll women in lesbian folklore is significant. These powerful and independent beings represent strength, resilience, and the ability to defy societal norms. They challenge the traditional gender roles and expectations, embodying a sense of freedom and self-acceptance. The presence of same-sex relationships within troll women stories adds another layer of inclusivity and representation in Nordic folklore.

For lesbian individuals, the stories of troll women can serve as a source of inspiration and empowerment. They provide a sense of validation and recognition, showcasing that love and relationships can exist beyond the boundaries of societal norms. These tales remind us that love knows no limits and that diverse forms of love should be celebrated and embraced.

In conclusion, while the stories of troll women in Nordic

folklore may not explicitly mention same-sex relationships, there are subtle hints and interpretations that suggest the presence of lesbian love within these tales. The emotional depth and closeness between female characters, as well as the symbolism of troll women, provide a space for the exploration of diverse forms of love and relationships. These stories serve as a source of inspiration and empowerment for lesbian individuals, reminding us of the importance of inclusive representation in folklore.

6.3 Stories of Lesbian Troll Women

In the rich tapestry of Nordic folklore, troll women hold a prominent place. These mystical creatures, often depicted as large and grotesque, are known for their magical abilities and their connection to the natural world. While troll women are typically portrayed as malevolent beings, there are hidden tales that reveal their involvement in same-sex relationships, specifically lesbian love.

One such story is the tale of Greta and Ingrid, two troll women who lived deep in the forests of Norway. Greta was known for her strength and cunning, while Ingrid possessed a gentle and compassionate nature. The two trolls met one fateful night during the summer solstice, when the boundaries between the human and troll realms were said to be the thinnest.

As Greta and Ingrid spent more time together, their friendship blossomed into something deeper. They found solace and understanding in each other's company, and their love grew stronger with each passing day. The forest became their sanctuary, a place where they could be themselves without fear of judgment or persecution.

Their love story, however, was not without its challenges. The troll community, steeped in tradition and prejudice, did not accept same-sex relationships. Greta and Ingrid faced ridicule and scorn from their fellow trolls, who saw their love as unnatural and forbidden. Despite the hardships they faced, the two troll women remained steadfast in their love for each other.

In one particularly poignant moment, Greta and Ingrid stumbled upon a hidden waterfall deep within the forest. The waterfall was said to possess magical properties, capable of granting wishes to those who truly believed. With hope in their hearts, the two troll women made a wish for acceptance and understanding from their community.

To their surprise, their wish was granted. The troll community, witnessing the depth of Greta and Ingrid's love, began to question their own prejudices. Slowly but surely, the walls of intolerance began to crumble, and same-sex relationships among trolls became more accepted.

Greta and Ingrid's love story became a symbol of hope and resilience for the troll community. Their tale spread far and wide, inspiring other troll women who were hiding their true selves to embrace their identities and seek love and happiness.

Another story of lesbian troll women comes from the folklore of Sweden. In this tale, two troll sisters named Astrid and Freja lived in the depths of a dark and mysterious forest. Astrid was known for her fiery spirit and adventurous nature, while Freja possessed a gentle and nurturing soul.

The bond between Astrid and Freja was unbreakable. They shared everything, from their deepest secrets to their wildest dreams. As they grew older, their friendship evolved into a love that surpassed all boundaries. They became inseparable, their lives intertwined like the roots of the ancient trees that surrounded them.

Their love was not without its challenges, however. The troll community, much like in the previous story, held deep-rooted prejudices against same-sex relationships. Astrid and Freja faced constant judgment and discrimination from their fellow trolls, who saw their love as a threat to tradition.

Despite the adversity they faced, Astrid and Freja remained true to themselves and their love. They found solace in the forest, where they could be free from the prying eyes and harsh words of others. The forest became their sanctuary, a place where they could express their love openly and without fear.

As time went on, Astrid and Freja's love story became a legend among the troll community. Their unwavering commitment to each other inspired other troll women to embrace their true selves and seek love and happiness, regardless of societal expectations.

The stories of Greta and Ingrid, as well as Astrid and Freja, are just a glimpse into the hidden tales of lesbian troll women in Nordic folklore. These stories serve as a reminder that love knows no boundaries and that true happiness can be found when we embrace our authentic selves.

Through these tales, we can see the power of representation and the importance of inclusivity in folklore. By exploring and sharing these hidden stories, we can inspire future generations to embrace diversity and celebrate love in all its forms. The stories of lesbian troll women remind us

6.4 The Symbolism of Troll Women in Lesbian Folklore

Troll women hold a significant place in Nordic folklore, often portrayed as powerful and mysterious beings. In lesbian folklore, troll women have come to symbolize strength, resilience, and the ability to defy societal norms. Their representation in lesbian folklore serves as a powerful metaphor for the experiences and struggles faced by lesbian women in Nordic societies.

Troll women are often depicted as independent and self-reliant, living in remote and secluded areas such as caves or deep forests. This isolation can be seen as a reflection of the isolation that lesbian women may feel in a society that often marginalizes and stigmatizes their identities. Just as troll women find solace and strength in their solitude, lesbian women find empowerment in embracing their true selves, even in the face of societal pressures.

One of the key aspects of troll women in lesbian folklore is their defiance of traditional gender roles and expectations. In Nordic societies, women were often expected to conform to societal norms and fulfill specific roles. However, troll women challenge these norms by embodying traits and characteristics that are traditionally associated with masculinity. They are often depicted as physically strong, assertive, and unapologetically themselves. This defiance of gender norms resonates with lesbian women who also challenge societal expectations by embracing their own identities and relationships.

The symbolism of troll women in lesbian folklore extends beyond their defiance of gender roles. They also represent a rejection of heteronormativity and the idea that love and relationships should only exist between a man and a woman. Troll women are often portrayed as having same-sex relationships or engaging in same-sex encounters. These stories serve as a powerful affirmation of lesbian love and desire, challenging the notion that same-sex relationships are unnatural or deviant.

Furthermore, troll women in lesbian folklore are often depicted as protectors and guardians of nature. They have a deep connection with the natural world and are seen as caretakers of the environment. This connection between troll women and nature can be seen as a reflection of the deep bond that lesbian women often have with the natural world. Many lesbian women find solace and a sense of belonging in nature, and the representation of troll women as guardians of the environment resonates with this connection.

In addition to their symbolism in lesbian folklore, troll women also play a role in empowering lesbian women to embrace their identities and find strength in their communities. Troll women are often portrayed as part of a larger community of magical beings, such as other trolls or forest spirits. This sense of community and belonging is crucial for lesbian women who may face isolation and discrimination in their everyday lives. The representation of troll women as part of a larger community sends a powerful message of solidarity and support, reminding lesbian women that they are not alone in their experiences.

In conclusion, troll women hold a significant place in lesbian folklore, symbolizing strength, resilience, and defiance of societal norms. Their representation in lesbian folklore serves as a powerful metaphor for the experiences and struggles faced by lesbian women in Nordic societies. Through their defiance of traditional gender roles, rejection of heteronormativity, and connection with nature, troll women empower lesbian women to embrace their identities and find strength in their communities. The symbolism of troll women in lesbian folklore continues to inspire and resonate with lesbian women, offering a sense of belonging, empowerment, and pride in their identities.

7

Chapter 7

The Witch Women

7.1 Understanding the Witch Women in Nordic Folklore

In Nordic folklore, the figure of the witch woman holds a significant place. Often portrayed as powerful and mysterious, these women possess a deep connection to nature and magic. While the term "witch" may carry negative connotations in some cultures, in Nordic folklore, it is associated with wisdom, healing, and spiritual knowledge. These witch women play a crucial role in the hidden tales of lesbians in Nordic folklore.

The witch women in Nordic folklore are known by various names, such as "völva" or "seidkona." They are believed to possess supernatural abilities and are often consulted for their wisdom and foresight. These women have a deep understanding of the natural world and its energies, and they use their knowledge to heal, protect, and guide their communities.

In the context of lesbian representation in Nordic folklore, the witch women hold a special significance. They are often depicted as independent and free-spirited individuals who defy societal norms and expectations. Their connection to nature and their ability to harness its power resonates with the experiences of lesbian women, who have historically been marginalized and oppressed.

One of the most well-known witch women in Nordic folklore is the character of Freyja. Freyja is a goddess associated with love, beauty, and fertility. She is often depicted as a powerful sorceress who possesses the ability to shape-shift and control the forces of nature. Freyja's portrayal as a witch woman highlights the connection between magic, femininity, and same-sex love.

In the hidden tales of lesbians in Nordic folklore, the witch women often form intimate relationships with other women. These relationships are portrayed as natural and accepted within their communities. The stories depict the deep emotional and spiritual connections between these women, emphasizing the beauty and strength of same-sex love.

One such tale is the story of Agnetha and Astrid, two witch women who lived in a small village nestled in the Nordic forests. Agnetha and Astrid were known for their healing abilities and their deep love for each other. They lived together in a cottage at the edge of the village, where they practiced their craft and cared for those in need.

Their love was celebrated by the villagers, who recognized the power and harmony that existed between them. Agnetha and Astrid's relationship was seen as a symbol of love and acceptance, challenging the traditional notions of gender and sexuality. Their story serves as a reminder of the inclusive and accepting nature of Nordic folklore.

The witch women in Nordic folklore also symbolize the

strength and resilience of lesbian women. They are often portrayed as independent and self-reliant, unafraid to challenge societal norms and expectations. Their connection to magic and nature represents their ability to tap into their own inner power and embrace their true selves.

Furthermore, the witch women in Nordic folklore serve as icons of lesbian culture. Their stories and representations provide a sense of belonging and validation for lesbian individuals, who often struggle to find themselves reflected in mainstream narratives. These tales offer a rich tapestry of lesbian experiences, showcasing the diversity and beauty of same-sex love.

In conclusion, the witch women in Nordic folklore play a vital role in the hidden tales of lesbians. They embody the power, wisdom, and resilience of lesbian women, challenging societal norms and embracing their true selves. Their stories provide a sense of belonging and validation for lesbian individuals, inspiring future generations to embrace their identities and celebrate their love. The witch women in Nordic folklore are not just characters in stories; they are symbols of strength, love, and acceptance.

7.2 Witch Women and Same-Sex Love

In Nordic folklore, the figure of the witch woman holds a significant place. Often portrayed as powerful and mysterious, these women possess a deep connection to nature and magic. They are known for their ability to cast spells, brew potions, and communicate with spirits. While the witch woman is often depicted as a solitary figure, she also forms bonds with other women, including same-sex relationships.

The representation of same-sex love in the context of witch women in Nordic folklore is intriguing and sheds light on the acceptance and recognition of lesbian relationships in ancient societies. These tales challenge the notion that homosexuality is a modern phenomenon and highlight the existence of diverse sexual orientations throughout history.

In many stories, witch women are shown to form deep emotional and romantic connections with other women. These relationships are often portrayed as loving and supportive, emphasizing the strength and resilience of lesbian love. The bond between witch women is depicted as a source of power, enabling them to harness their magical abilities and navigate the challenges they face.

One such tale is the story of Freya and Gerda, two witch women who lived in a secluded forest. Freya was known for her ability to control the elements, while Gerda possessed the gift of healing. They met during a gathering of witches and immediately felt a strong connection. As they spent more time together, their friendship blossomed into a deep love.

Their relationship was not without obstacles, as they faced prejudice and discrimination from those who did not understand or accept their love. However, Freya and Gerda remained steadfast in their commitment to each other, finding solace and strength in their shared experiences as witch women. Together, they used their magic to protect their community and challenge the societal norms that sought to suppress their love.

Another tale tells the story of Ingrid and Astrid, two witch women who lived in a small village. Ingrid was known for her ability to communicate with animals, while Astrid possessed the power of divination. They were drawn to each other by their shared love for nature and their desire to use their magic for the greater good.

As their friendship deepened, Ingrid and Astrid realized that their connection went beyond friendship. They fell in love and embraced their lesbian identity, finding comfort and acceptance in each other's arms. Together, they used their magic to heal the sick, protect the vulnerable, and fight against injustice.

These tales of lesbian witch women in Nordic folklore challenge the stereotypes and misconceptions surrounding same-sex love. They depict lesbian relationships as natural and beautiful, emphasizing the importance of love and acceptance in society. The witch women in these stories serve as powerful symbols of resilience, empowerment, and the celebration of diversity.

The representation of lesbian relationships in Nordic folklore not only provides a historical perspective on same-sex love but also offers a sense of validation and belonging to lesbian individuals today. By acknowledging and celebrating these hidden tales, we can inspire and empower future generations to embrace their identities and love without fear or shame.

In conclusion, the representation of witch women in Nordic folklore provides a fascinating insight into the acceptance and recognition of same-sex love in ancient societies. These tales challenge societal norms and celebrate the beauty and power of lesbian relationships. By exploring and sharing these hidden tales, we can inspire a more inclusive and accepting future for all.

7.3 Tales of Lesbian Witch Women

In Nordic folklore, the figure of the witch woman holds a significant place. Often portrayed as powerful and mysterious, these women possess magical abilities and are deeply connected to nature and the spiritual realm. While the tales of witch women in Nordic folklore predominantly focus on their interactions with otherworldly beings and their role as healers or seers, there are also hidden tales that explore their relationships with other women, including same-sex love.

One such tale is the story of Freya, a renowned witch woman who lived deep in the forests of Norway. Freya was known for her exceptional magical abilities and her deep connection to the spirits of the land. She was revered by the local community for her healing powers and her wisdom. However, there were whispers among the villagers about Freya's secret love for another woman, Astrid.

Astrid was a young and beautiful woman who lived in the nearby village. She was drawn to Freya's enchanting presence and sought her guidance in matters of the heart. As their friendship grew, so did their love for each other. They would often meet in secret, hidden away from prying eyes, deep in the heart of the forest. Their love blossomed amidst the whispers of the trees and the gentle caress of the wind.

Together, Freya and Astrid would embark on magical journeys, exploring the hidden realms of the supernatural. They would dance under the moonlight, casting spells and invoking ancient spirits. Their love was a source of strength and power, fueling their magical abilities and deepening their connection to the natural world.

However, their love was not without challenges. The villagers, steeped in superstition and fear, began to suspect Freya and Astrid's relationship. Rumors spread like wildfire, and soon the couple found themselves facing hostility and prejudice. The villagers accused them of practicing dark magic and branded them as witches.

Despite the persecution they faced, Freya and Astrid remained steadfast in their love for each other. They refused to let the ignorance of others extinguish the flame that burned within their hearts. They continued to practice their craft, using their magic to protect themselves and those who sought their help.

In another tale, there is the story of Ingrid, a witch woman who lived in the remote mountains of Sweden. Ingrid was known for her ability to communicate with animals and her deep knowledge of herbal remedies. She was a solitary figure, preferring the company of her animal companions over that of humans. However, her solitude was broken when she encountered Greta, a young woman who had lost her way in the mountains.

Greta was captivated by Ingrid's mystical aura and sought her guidance to find her way back home. Ingrid, sensing a kindred spirit in Greta, took her under her wing and taught her the ways of magic and healing. As their bond grew stronger, so did their love for each other. They found solace in each other's arms, their love becoming a sanctuary in the midst of the harsh mountain landscape.

Together, Ingrid and Greta would embark on magical adventures, using their powers to protect the natural world from harm. They would commune with the spirits of the mountains, seeking their guidance and wisdom. Their love was a testament to the strength and resilience of the human spirit, transcending societal norms and expectations.

These tales of lesbian witch women in Nordic folklore highlight the hidden narratives of love and companionship that exist within the realm of magic and mythology. They challenge the traditional narratives of folklore, which often focus on heterosexual relationships, and provide a glimpse into the diverse experiences of women in Nordic culture.

These stories serve as a reminder that love knows no boundaries and that the power of love can transcend societal norms and expectations. They celebrate the strength and resilience of lesbian women in the face of adversity and inspire us to embrace our true selves, regardless of the judgments of others.

The tales of lesbian witch women in Nordic folklore are a testament to the richness and diversity of human experiences. They remind us of the importance of inclusivity and representation in folklore, allowing marginalized voices to be heard and celebrated. By exploring these hidden tales, we can inspire future generations to embrace their identities and find solace in the stories that reflect their own experiences.

7.4 The Witch Women as Icons of Lesbian Culture

Throughout Nordic folklore, the figure of the witch woman has been a prominent and complex character. Often portrayed as powerful, mysterious, and independent, the witch woman has captivated the imaginations of many. In the context of lesbian culture, the witch woman has taken on a special significance, becoming an icon of strength, resilience, and sexual liberation.

In Nordic folklore, the witch woman is often depicted as a solitary figure who possesses magical abilities and a deep connection to nature. She is seen as a healer, a seer, and a guardian of ancient wisdom. However, she is also feared and misunderstood by the wider society, often being accused of practicing dark magic and consorting with evil spirits. This duality of the witch woman's character mirrors the experiences of many lesbians throughout history.

Lesbian women, like the witch woman, have often been marginalized and persecuted by society due to their sexual orientation. They have been labeled as deviant, immoral, and dangerous. Just as the witch woman was accused of practicing dark magic, lesbians have been accused of corrupting societal norms and threatening the established order. This parallel between the witch woman and lesbian women has led to the witch woman becoming an important symbol of lesbian culture.

In lesbian folklore and literature, the witch woman is often portrayed as a rebel who defies societal expectations and embraces her true self. She is a symbol of empowerment and liberation, challenging the patriarchal structures that seek to suppress and control women's sexuality. The witch woman's association with magic and the supernatural also reflects the hidden and mysterious nature of lesbian desire, which has often been relegated to the shadows.

One example of a lesbian witch woman in Nordic folklore is the character of Gryla. In Icelandic mythology, Gryla is a fearsome ogress who lives in the mountains and preys on misbehaving children. However, in some interpretations, Gryla is also depicted as a powerful sorceress who forms a coven of women and engages in same-sex relationships. This portrayal of Gryla as a lesbian witch woman highlights the subversive and empowering nature of lesbian desire.

Another example is the character of Frau Holle in Germanic folklore. Frau Holle is a wise and powerful witch who controls the weather and rewards those who are kind and hardworking. In some versions of the story, Frau Holle is depicted as having a female companion, suggesting a same-sex relationship. This portrayal of Frau Holle as a lesbian witch woman challenges traditional gender roles and celebrates the love between women.

In contemporary lesbian culture, the witch woman has become an important symbol of resistance and self-acceptance. Lesbian witches, often referred to as "queer witches," embrace their connection to nature, magic, and the divine feminine. They draw inspiration from the witch woman archetype to reclaim their power and challenge societal norms. Through rituals, spells, and community gatherings, lesbian witches create spaces of inclusivity, healing, and empowerment.

The witch woman's association with lesbian culture also extends to the realm of fashion and aesthetics. Many lesbians embrace a witchy style, characterized by flowing dresses, dark colors, and mystical accessories. This aesthetic is a visual representation of their connection to the witch woman archetype and serves as a form of self-expression and identity.

In conclusion, the witch woman in Nordic folklore has become an icon of lesbian culture, representing strength, resilience, and sexual liberation. Just as the witch woman defies societal expectations and embraces her true self, lesbian women have fought against marginalization and discrimination to live authentically. The witch woman's association with magic, nature, and the supernatural reflects the hidden and mysterious nature of lesbian desire. Through embracing the witch woman archetype, lesbian women reclaim their power, challenge societal norms, and inspire future generations to embrace their true selves.

8

Chapter 8

Conclusion

8.1 The Importance of Inclusive Folklore

Folklore plays a significant role in shaping cultural identity and preserving historical narratives. It reflects the beliefs, values, and traditions of a society, providing a window into the past and offering insights into the lives of its people. However, for far too long, certain voices and experiences have been marginalized or excluded from traditional folklore. In recent years, there has been a growing recognition of the importance of inclusive folklore, which encompasses diverse perspectives and narratives. This chapter explores the significance of inclusive folklore, particularly in relation to the representation of lesbians in Nordic folklore.

Preserving Hidden Histories

Inclusive folklore is crucial for preserving hidden histories and ensuring that all members of society feel seen and heard. By uncovering and sharing the stories of lesbians in Nordic folklore, we can shed light on a previously overlooked aspect of cultural heritage. These hidden tales provide a valuable insight into the lives and experiences of lesbians in the past, allowing us to better understand their contributions to society and their struggles against societal norms.

Challenging Stereotypes and Assumptions

Inclusive folklore challenges stereotypes and assumptions about gender and sexuality. By including stories of lesbian characters in Nordic folklore, we can disrupt the heteronormative narrative that has dominated traditional folklore for centuries. This representation helps to normalize same-sex relationships and validates the experiences of lesbians, fostering a more inclusive and accepting society.

Empowering Lesbian Communities

Representation in folklore can have a profound impact on marginalized communities, including lesbians. When lesbians see themselves reflected in the stories and myths of their culture, it can provide a sense of validation and empowerment. Inclusive folklore allows lesbians to connect with their cultural heritage and find strength in the knowledge that their experiences are not only valid but also celebrated.

Building Bridges Across Generations

Inclusive folklore has the power to bridge the gap between generations and foster understanding and acceptance. By sharing stories of lesbians in Nordic folklore, we can create a dialogue between older generations who may have grown up with traditional folklore and younger generations who are seeking more diverse and inclusive narratives. This exchange of stories and perspectives can help to break down barriers and promote empathy and understanding.

Inspiring Creativity and Imagination

Inclusive folklore sparks creativity and imagination by offering new narratives and perspectives. By including stories of lesbians in Nordic folklore, we open up a world of possibilities for writers, artists, and creators to explore and reimagine these tales. This creative engagement with inclusive folklore not only enriches the cultural landscape but also allows for the development of new stories and art that reflect the diversity of human experiences.

Fostering Social Change

Inclusive folklore has the potential to foster social change by challenging societal norms and promoting acceptance and equality. By including stories of lesbians in Nordic folklore, we can contribute to the ongoing fight for LGBTQ+ rights and visibility. These stories serve as a reminder that same-sex love and relationships have always existed and are an integral part of human history. By acknowledging and celebrating this history, we can work towards a more inclusive and equitable society.

Conclusion

Inclusive folklore is essential for preserving hidden histories, challenging stereotypes, empowering marginalized communities, building bridges across generations, inspiring creativity, and fostering social change. By exploring the hidden tales of lesbians in Nordic folklore, we can contribute to a more inclusive understanding of our cultural heritage. It is through the recognition and celebration of diverse narratives that we can create a more accepting and inclusive society for all.

8.2 The Power of Lesbian Representation in Nordic Folklore

Lesbian representation in Nordic folklore holds immense power in shaping narratives, challenging societal norms, and providing a sense of belonging and validation for the LGBTQ+ community. By exploring hidden tales of lesbians in Nordic folklore, we can uncover the rich history of same-sex love and relationships that have often been overlooked or marginalized.

Throughout history, folklore has served as a reflection of societal values, beliefs, and experiences. It has the ability to both reinforce and challenge existing norms, making it a powerful tool for social change. By including lesbian characters and stories in Nordic folklore, we can challenge heteronormative narratives and create a more inclusive understanding of love and relationships.

One of the significant aspects of lesbian representation in Nordic folklore is the validation it provides for individuals who identify as lesbian. Seeing oneself reflected in stories and legends can be a transformative experience, offering a sense of acceptance and normalcy. It allows lesbians to feel seen, heard, and understood, fostering a sense of pride and self-acceptance.

Lesbian representation in Nordic folklore also has the power to challenge and subvert traditional gender roles and expectations. In many traditional tales, women are often portrayed as passive, submissive, and dependent on male characters. By introducing lesbian characters who defy these stereotypes, folklore can challenge the notion that women exist solely for the pleasure and companionship of men. It empowers women to embrace their own desires and forge their own paths, free from societal expectations.

Furthermore, lesbian representation in Nordic folklore can help dismantle the harmful myth that same-sex love is a modern phenomenon or a product of Western influence. By uncovering hidden tales of lesbians in Nordic folklore, we can demonstrate that same-sex love has existed across cultures and throughout history. This challenges the notion that homosexuality is a foreign concept or a result of contemporary social changes. It affirms the existence and validity of lesbian relationships in Nordic societies, providing a historical context for contemporary LGBTQ+ experiences.

Lesbian representation in Nordic folklore also has the potential to foster empathy and understanding among non-LGBTQ+ individuals. By humanizing lesbian characters and portraying their experiences with depth and complexity, folklore can challenge stereotypes and prejudices. It allows readers to connect with lesbian characters on an emotional level, promoting empathy and compassion. This can lead to greater acceptance and support for the LGBTQ+ community as a whole.

Moreover, lesbian representation in Nordic folklore can inspire and empower future generations. By showcasing strong, resilient, and courageous lesbian characters, folklore can provide role models for young LGBTQ+ individuals. It offers a vision of possibility and hope, showing that lesbian love and relationships are not only valid but also worthy of celebration. This representation can help young LGBTQ+ individuals navigate their own identities and find the strength to embrace their true selves.

In conclusion, the power of lesbian representation in Nordic folklore cannot be underestimated. By including lesbian characters and stories, folklore has the ability to challenge societal norms, provide validation for the LGBTQ+ community, dismantle harmful stereotypes, foster empathy and understanding, and inspire future generations. It is through the exploration of hidden tales of lesbians in Nordic folklore that we can create a more inclusive and accepting society, where all individuals are seen, heard, and celebrated for who they are.

8.3 Continuing the Exploration of Hidden Tales

Throughout this book, we have delved into the rich and enchanting world of Nordic folklore, uncovering the hidden tales of lesbians that have long been overlooked. We have explored the stories of Valkyries, Norns, Sea Maidens, Forest Spirits, Troll Women, and Witch Women, discovering the presence of same-sex love and relationships within these mythical beings. As we conclude our exploration, it is important to recognize the significance of continuing to uncover and share these hidden tales.

Nordic folklore is a vast and diverse tapestry of stories, passed down through generations, and deeply rooted in the cultural fabric of the Nordic countries. While we have touched upon the representation of women in Nordic folklore in Section 1.3, it is crucial to acknowledge that the exploration of lesbian narratives within this folklore is still in its infancy. There is much more to be discovered and shared, and it is our responsibility as scholars, storytellers, and enthusiasts to continue this exploration.

By continuing to uncover hidden tales of lesbians in Nordic folklore, we not only shed light on the experiences and identities of lesbian individuals in the past, but we also contribute to the broader understanding of LGBTQ+ history and culture. These stories provide a glimpse into the lives of lesbian women in a time when their existence was often marginalized or erased. They offer a sense of validation and representation for lesbian individuals today, reminding them that their identities have always been a part of the human experience.

Moreover, the exploration of hidden tales allows us to challenge and disrupt the heteronormative narratives that have dominated folklore for centuries. By highlighting the presence of same-sex love and relationships within these mythical beings, we challenge the notion that such relationships are modern or unnatural. We affirm that love and desire between women have always existed, even if they were not always openly acknowledged or celebrated.

Continuing the exploration of hidden tales also opens up avenues for further research and scholarship. As we uncover more stories and delve deeper into the nuances of lesbian representation in Nordic folklore, we can gain a more comprehensive understanding of the diverse experiences and identities within the LGBTQ+ community. This research can contribute to academic fields such as folklore studies, gender studies, and queer studies, enriching our knowledge and challenging existing frameworks.

Furthermore, the exploration of hidden tales has the power to inspire and empower future generations. By bringing these stories to light, we provide lesbian individuals with a sense of belonging and pride in their heritage. Young readers who identify as lesbian can see themselves reflected in these tales, finding solace and strength in knowing that their stories are not only valid but also celebrated. By including lesbian narratives in the folklore canon, we create a more inclusive and diverse cultural landscape for all.

In order to continue the exploration of hidden tales, it is essential to support and amplify the voices of marginalized communities. This includes seeking out and listening to the stories and experiences of lesbian individuals within the Nordic countries and beyond. It involves engaging with LGBTQ+ organizations, scholars, and activists who are working tirelessly to uncover and preserve these narratives. By collaborating and sharing resources, we can ensure that the exploration of hidden tales becomes a collective effort, driven by a commitment to inclusivity and representation.

In conclusion, the exploration of hidden tales of lesbians in Nordic folklore is an ongoing journey that holds immense value and significance. By continuing to uncover and share these stories, we contribute to the broader understanding of LGBTQ+ history, challenge heteronormative narratives, inspire future generations, and create a more inclusive cultural landscape. Let us embrace the power of storytelling and continue to celebrate the hidden tales that have been waiting to be discovered.

8.4 Inspiring Future Generations through Lesbian Folklore

Lesbian folklore in Nordic culture holds immense power in inspiring future generations. By exploring and sharing these hidden tales, we can create a sense of belonging, empowerment, and validation for lesbian individuals. These stories not only provide representation but also serve as a reminder of the rich diversity within Nordic folklore.

Lesbian folklore offers a unique perspective on love, relationships, and identity. It challenges traditional narratives and expands the boundaries of what is considered acceptable or normal. By showcasing lesbian characters in these tales, we can challenge societal norms and promote inclusivity.

One of the most significant aspects of lesbian folklore is its ability to provide role models for young lesbians who may be struggling with their own identities. These stories offer a sense of hope and possibility, showing that lesbian love and relationships have always existed and are just as valid as any other.

Through lesbian folklore, we can also educate future generations about the history and contributions of lesbian individuals in Nordic culture. By highlighting the stories of lesbian Valkyries, Norns, Sea Maidens, Forest Spirits, Troll Women, and Witch Women, we can shed light on the often overlooked and marginalized experiences of lesbian individuals throughout history.

These tales can serve as a source of inspiration and empowerment for young lesbians, helping them to embrace their identities and find strength in their own stories. By seeing themselves reflected in these narratives, they can develop a sense of pride and self-acceptance.

Furthermore, lesbian folklore can foster a sense of community and connection among lesbian individuals. By sharing these stories, we create a space for dialogue and understanding, allowing lesbians to connect with each other and find solace in shared experiences. This sense of community is crucial in combating feelings of isolation and promoting a sense of belonging.

In addition to inspiring future generations of lesbians, lesbian folklore can also educate and raise awareness among non-lesbian individuals. By exposing them to these stories, we can challenge stereotypes and misconceptions, fostering empathy and understanding. This can lead to greater acceptance and support for lesbian individuals within society.

It is important to continue the exploration and preservation of lesbian folklore for future generations. By documenting and sharing these stories, we ensure that they are not lost or forgotten. This can be done through various mediums such as books, films, art, and digital platforms. By making lesbian folklore accessible and visible, we can ensure that future generations have the opportunity to engage with and be inspired by these tales.

Furthermore, it is essential to encourage the creation of new lesbian folklore. By supporting and promoting the work of contemporary lesbian authors, artists, and storytellers, we can ensure that lesbian voices continue to be heard and celebrated. This can be done through grants, scholarships, and mentorship programs that specifically focus on supporting lesbian creators.

By inspiring future generations through lesbian folklore, we can create a more inclusive and accepting society. These stories have the power to challenge norms, provide representation, foster a sense of community, and educate both lesbians and non-lesbians alike. Through the exploration and preservation of lesbian folklore, we can ensure that the voices and experiences of lesbian individuals are celebrated and valued for generations to come.

Afterword

These hidden tales, while shrouded in the mists of time, are a testament to the enduring resilience of love, transcending cultural boundaries and echoing through the ages. In these narratives, we witness love's ability to challenge norms, defy expectations, and flourish even in the face of adversity.

My quest to uncover these stories was not without its challenges, for the history of LGBTQ+ representation in folklore is a complex and evolving tapestry. Yet, it is precisely this complexity that makes our journey all the more vital. It reminds us that stories, like love, are multifaceted, shaped by the cultural norms and societal contexts of their time.

We hope that this book has provided a glimpse into the richness of Nordic folklore, while honoring the voices and experiences that have been overlooked for far too long. It serves as a call to embrace diversity and inclusivity in the world of myth and legend, as we recognize that the stories we tell are reflections of the human experience itself.

Let's carry forward these hidden tales in our hearts, reminding us that love, in all its forms, has always had a place in the timeless stories of the North.

With gratitude for taking the journey through these hidden tales,

Sara